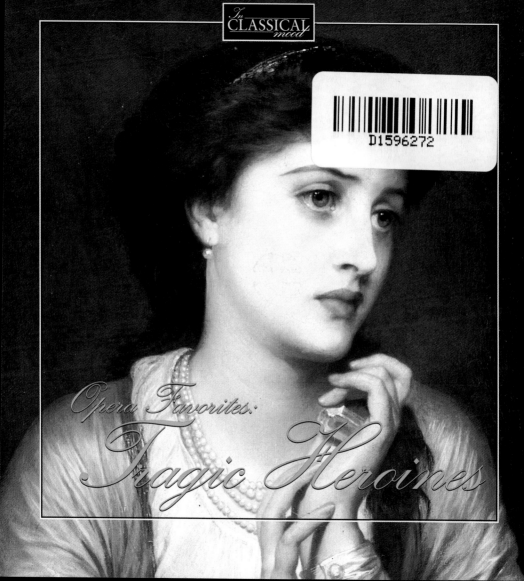

In CLASSICAL mood

D1596272

Opera Favorites:
Tragic Heroines

Tragic Heroines

*S*ome of opera's most famous and touching music has been written to express the plight of women at the mercy of their destiny or society. In each of the three operas featured in *Tragic Heroines*, the heroine is an attractive and noble character, whose happiness and fulfillment cannot be achieved in this world. In Verdi's *La Traviata*, Violetta, the tragic "lost woman" of the title, has her happiness destroyed by the hypocritical morality of Parisian society. Puccini's tender Mimì in *La Bohème* leads an independent life as a working girl, but ultimately dies, wasted away by tuberculosis brought on by her wretched circumstances. And in *Lucia di Lammermoor*, Donizetti portrays—in one of the most famous and heart-rending scenes in musical drama—his heroine's innocent mind deranged through family treachery.

WHAT THE SYMBOLS MEAN

THE COMPOSERS	THE MUSIC	THE STORY	THE INSPIRATION	THE BACKGROUND
Their lives... their loves... their legacies...	Explanation... analysis... interpretation...	The plot of the opera, act by act	How works of genius came to be written	People, places, and events linked to the music

© MCMXCVIII IMP AB   In Classical Mood™   IMP AB, produced under license by IMP Inc.   Printed in China.   US P 2201 12 050

Contents

La Traviata

GIUSEPPE VERDI *1813–1901*

*V*ioletta, the "traviata" of the title, is the woman led astray or rather a high-class prostitute. Yet, Violetta reveals herself as a "flower" of great and unusual worth, her somewhat sleazy lifestyle redeemed by her loving and noble character.

AHEAD OF ITS TIME

Verdi and his librettist, Francesco Maria Piave, based *La Traviata* on *La Dame aux camélias* by Alexandre Dumas the Younger. The opera was well ahead of its time, and unique among Verdi's works. For the first time, he intended the setting and characters to be contemporary rather than historical, which made the subject seem particularly scandalous. Through Violetta (*right*), conventional morality is reversed, for she is a courtesan with a fine character. Respectable values, by contrast, appear self-seeking and callous. This was clearly too much for genteel audiences to stomach, and for many years the setting was distanced back to the 1700s. However, *La Traviata* was still seen as an attack on marriage, although many saw it as a powerful argument for "illict," but true, love. Quite apart from the controversial subject matter, inital performances of *La Traviata* were also dogged by casting problems. Verdi had serious misgivings about the three main singers, and voiced his concerns in a letter to the management of Venice's La Fenice opera house, but no action was taken. Verdi was understandably distraught, but his work soon transformed from a first-night disaster into one of the true opera greats.

A Dangerous Liaison

*L*iving in Paris in 1850, Violetta is a beautiful courtesan, but she is not acceptable in polite society. However, when she falls in love for the first time, she shows herself to be more noble and dignified than any of her more respectable contemporaries.

PRINCIPAL CHARACTERS

Violetta Valéry: a courtesan; **Alfredo Germont:** her lover; **Giorgio Germont:** Alfredo's father; **Flora Bervoix:** Violetta's friend; **Baron Douphol:** Violetta's elderly protector; **Dr. Grenvil:** Violetta's doctor; **Annina:** Violetta's maid

BRIEF ENCOUNTER

ACT I

Violetta is holding a party (*left*) to celebrate a return to better health after a bout of tuberculosis. A friend introduces her to Alfredo, a young man who has called every day during her illness to ask after her. She invites her guests to begin the dance in an adjoining room, but not feeling well, she stays behind. Alfredo remains with her and takes the opportunity to declare his love and his desire to look after her. Violetta warns him it is dangerous to love her, for she is too cold and brittle for such true feelings. She dismisses him but invites him to return the next day. Alone after her guests' departure, she wonders if Alfredo might be the ideal lover she has always dreamed of, but decides it is her destiny to live and die in the glittering whirl of Parisian high life.

AN UNWELCOME VISITOR

ACT II Months later, Alfredo and Violetta are living idyllically in the country. While Alfredo is away on business, his father, Giorgio Germont, arrives. He convinces Violetta (*left*) that the scandal of their liaison is ruining his daughter's marriage prospects and destroying Alfredo's own future, so she must leave him. Heartbroken, Violetta finally gives in, asking Giorgio to reveal the reason for her apparent betrayal after her death. When Alfredo returns, Violetta passionately begs him to love her, then flees. But he finds a note from her and pursues her, despite the protests of his father.

In the next scene, Violetta has returned to her former lover, Baron Douphol, and is at a party thrown by her friend, Flora. Alfredo arrives in a reckless mood and beats the Baron at cards. When Violetta refuses to leave with Alfredo, and pretends to love the Baron, Alfredo calls the guests as witnesses and throws his winnings at her in payment for their time together. Violetta faints, and Germont arrives, joining in the general consternation, while the Baron challenges Alfredo to a duel.

LAST HOURS

ACT III Weeks later, Violetta is desperately ill, looked after only by her maid, Annina. Unknown to her, she has just a few hours to live. She reads a letter from Giorgio Germont, telling her that Alfredo now knows of her sacrifice, and wants to visit her. He arrives and throws himself into Violetta's arms, begging her forgiveness. She appears to rally, and together they plan a future together away from Paris. As Germont, Annina and Dr. Grenvil appear, Violetta breathes her last breath, cradled in her lover's arms.

Champagne and Tears

PRELUDE

1 Swooning strings—melancholic, romantic, yearning—provide the introduction to the opera. Boldly, Verdi opens his work with music from the last act, which foreshadows the death of Violetta. In doing this, he establishes her personality and fate as the very foundation on which the opera is based. A second theme, on cellos, unfolds with a gentle rhythmic accompaniment, preparing the scene for the bustle of the sophisticated party on which the curtain rises.

UN DÌ FELICE, ETEREA

2 When Violetta is alone with Alfredo at her party (*below*), he tells her how, since "one happy, ethereal day," he has loved her with a love that is the very pulse of the universe. The touching melody reflects the depth and sincerity of his feelings and his own wonderment at the mysterious power of love. She replies with a nervous, jerky version of his tune, showing she is both moved by, yet fearful of, such a declaration. She can only offer friendship, so he must find another to love.

FOLLIE! FOLLIE! ... SEMPRE LIBERA

3 Alone, Violetta reveals her true isolation. Can Alfredo bring her true love? In this famous aria, she muses it is "folly" to entertain the thought. She must be "always free," flitting from pleasure to pleasure. But she is clearly affected by him, for the the sound of his words breaks in on her thoughts, and she tries to drown her awakening feelings by reflecting on her hectic life of pleasure.

PURA SICCOME UN ANGELO

TRACK 4 ACT II Alfredo's father has come to persuade Violetta to give up her liaison with his son (*left*). The older Germont tries to touch her heart by describing the innocence and beauty of his daughter, Alfredo's younger sister, "pure as an angel." The young man who loves this girl, and is loved in return, will not marry her while her brother is involved in a scandalous love affair. At first, Violetta misinterprets him, thinking that she only has to leave Alfredo for a short time. When she realizes Germont means forever she is aghast. "No! Never!" she cries. "Can you not see what love I feel for him? I have no one else, no family, no friends." Alfredo swore to be everything to her. In desperation, she reveals her awful secret: she is wasting away with a terrible disease and the trauma of parting would surely kill her.

ALFREDO, ALFREDO, DI QUESTO CORE

TRACK 5 ACT II Thinking she has betrayed him, Alfredo insults Violetta in public. Recovering from a faint, she says, "Alfredo, in my heart" is a love he cannot fully understand. But, she continues, one day he will know why she has left him, and she prays he will not then feel remorse. Everyone gathers around, full of pity for her, and Alfredo is horrified at what he has done.

PARIGI, O CARA, NOI LASCEREMO

TRACK 6 ACT II Alfredo, returning to Violetta as she is dying, begs her forgiveness. He promises, "We will leave Paris, oh my darling," for the country. Here she will recover her health and the future will be good. They sing a beautiful duet (*right*), as if their hope is so strong that it briefly becomes reality.

Redeemed by Love

La Traviata is the third of the three great and ever-popular operas from Verdi's middle period—the early 1850s. Of the other two, *Rigoletto* proved a real breakthrough, as it was organized as a drama rather than a string of arias. And *Il Trovatore* has thrilled audiences since its premiere because of its fast pace, passion and variety of music. *La Traviata* is perhaps the most perfectly constructed of the three, each scene having its own momentum and atmosphere. The three operas also reveal Verdi's understanding of the nature of human relationships, expressed, for example, in Rigoletto's deep affection for his daughter and in Violetta's vulnerable and passionate love for Alfredo.

A Life Companion

The story of Verdi's *La Traviata* had a parallel in his own life. From 1847 he set up home with the charming Giuseppina Strepponi (*right*), one of the great singing actresses of her day. She had already enjoyed a hugely successful career from which she supported her family, including two illegitimate children. She championed and starred in Verdi's early operas, notably *Nabucco*, but her voice deteriorated early through overwork and she moved to Paris to teach. Here, she once again met Verdi, and they became lovers. Until they married in 1859, their life at his country house caused much local gossip and offended the father of Verdi's first wife, who had died some years before. Such reactions infuriated Verdi.

HEART OF THE OPERA

The confrontation between Giorgio Germont, Alfredo's father, and Violetta in Act II (*below*) is pivotal to the opera. Germont represents the full force of bourgeois morality, which can only accept sexual love within marriage. As he tries to persuade Violetta to give up her liaison with Alfredo, he becomes more and more impressed by her sincerity and takes no real pleasure in winning his point. For Violetta, he is also something of a father figure, whose opinion she must accept. By the end, the force and truth of her feelings prove stronger than convention, and his own rigid morality is softened by compassion and respect for her.

IN PERFORMANCE

A year after the disastrous premiere, Verdi agreed to another production of *La Traviata* at a different theater in Venice. It was wildly successful. Verdi wryly remarked that it was the same audience hearing the same music all over again. Since then, it has remained one of the world's five most performed operas and a favorite with divas from Maria Callas to Montserrat Caballé.

 K E Y   N O T E S

La Traviata is probably the first opera to feature death from tuberculosis. The disease reached epidemic proportions in the 19th century and was a terrible killer of young people. Verdi treats Violetta's condition realistically, giving stage directions drawing attention to her pallor and to her ecstatic death—a surge of energy that was a peculiar feature of the disease.

La Bohème

GIACOMO PUCCINI *1858-1924*

A youthful theme embellished with gorgeous tunes makes for the enduring appeal of *La Bohème*. The young artists are so sympathetic and believable that everyone can identify with their struggles. But, warm hearts and high spirits can't conquer poverty or tragedy.

A BOHEMIAN LIFE

The inspiration for *La Bohème* was a French novel, "Scenes from Bohemian Life" by Henri Murger in 1845. The writer, a struggling and impoverished hack, was depicting scenes from his own life. His "Bohemia" was not in Central Europe but in Paris: "bounded to the North by the cold, to the East by hunger, to the South by love and to the West by hope." When the stories were dramatized, Murger became quite rich. However, he came to feel that his fictionalized accounts gave a far too heroic impression of the Bohemian life, and he warned young people against it.

When Puccini discovered that Ruggero Leoncavallo was planning an opera based on the novel, he vowed to get there first. The process, however, was not entirely smooth. Although *La Bohème* opened to a lukewarm response in 1896, the opera soon became a favorite, fully justifying the faith Puccini had in it from the start.

In the Name of Love

In 1830s Paris, "to be five-and-twenty, poor and in love: that is enough." This could be the creed of the four Bohemians. With their working-girl sweethearts, they laugh and love their way through life, but find they must pay a price for keeping body and soul together.

SEASON'S GREETINGS

It is Christmas Eve and the impoverished Bohemians are freezing and starving in their garret (*below*). They are saved by Schaunard, who has been paid for assasinating an Englishman's parrot by his violin playing. He brings the money, along with food and wine, which is soon put to good use to trick their landlord out of the rent he has come to collect. Exhilerated by their good fortune, the men set off for the evening, but Rodolfo cannot join them yet—he has to finish an article. Uninspired and restless, he is delighted to find his neighbor, the fragile Mimi, knocking at the door to ask for a light for her candle. Overcome by a fit of coughing, she swoons into his arms. All Rodolfo's tender feelings are awakened and he persuades her to stay. As they talk about their lives and dreams, they realize they are falling in love. Blissfully happy, they set off to join the others.

ACT
I

PRINCIPAL CHARACTERS
Rodolfo: a poet;
Mimi: a seamstress, his lover;
Marcello: a painter;
Musetta: a singer, his lover;
Schaunard: a musician;
Colline: a philosopher

LAUGHTER, MUSIC AND SONG

Mimi and Rodolfo arrive at the Café Momus (*left*) to join the other Bohemians. The street is alive with festivity as children pester a toyseller, soldiers march to and fro and various hawkers call out their wares. Enter Musetta weighed down by her purchases, cutting a swathe through the bustle and escorted by Alcindoro, an elderly and conveniently rich admirer. Her lover, Marcello, is furious. But she has a ruse up her pretty sleeve. Making a scene over her shoe, she unabashedly draws attention to her charms, until Marcello can no longer resist her. He whisks her off in a passionate embrace and the others follow—leaving Alcindoro to settle their bill.

QUARRELS AND RECONCILIATIONS

Two months later, Mimi and Rodolfo, having quarrelled and parted the night before, meet up at the inn where Marcello now lives with Musetta. Unaware that Mimi is listening (*right*), Rodolfo breaks down and confesses to Marcello his fear that she is dying. Her coughing reveals Mimi, and the lovers are temporarily reconciled for the winter. Realizing they could never stay together, Mimi runs off in the spring with a wealthy, older man.

Act IV finds all the Bohemians back in the garret. Suddenly, Musetta rushes in—Mimi has collapsed in the street. She is brought inside and Colline is sent to fetch a doctor. But it is too late. She dies almost before the others realize what has happened.

Songs and Lovers

CHE GELIDA MANINA

(Track 7, Act 1) Mimi and Rodolfo's hands brush against each other in the dark. "Your tiny hand is frozen," he exclaims. "Let me warm it into life." He begins to tell her about himself. Although he is only an impoverished writer, with his castles in the air, he is a millionaire in spirit. However, he has been robbed by two thieves: her pretty eyes! Rising to a crescendo, he reveals his feelings and ideas until she is captivated. "And now, will you tell me about yourself?" he asks.

SÌ. MI CHIAMANO MIMI

(Track 8, Act 1) "Yes," she replies, "I am called Mimi," although her real name is Lucia. She makes her living creating artificial flowers and loves the simple things of life that speak of love, of spring, of such things that only poets know. She is content in her little white room, where the first rays of the spring sun arrive to coax a rose to bloom; but, alas, the flowers she fashions have no perfume. Mimi and Rodolfo have just met, but the music reveals their mutual attraction and gives a glimpse into their hopes and passions.

O SOAVE FANCIULLA

(Track 9, Act 1) Rodolfo, turning from the window, finds Mimi bathed in moonlight and is enchanted by the sight. "O lovely maiden," he sighs, "you are my dream come true." He wants her to stay with him, but she suggests that they go off and join his friends. The music swells to a climax, summing up their pent-up emotions, and then subsides as their final ecstatic notes die away.

QUANDO MEN VO

TRACK 10 ACT II Musetta is a minx, and unlike the coy Mimi, has other ways of getting her man. Her seduction is brazen and completely public. In this enchanting waltz, she literally parades her charms to regain the attention of the jealous Marcello. "When I step out," she declares, "the whole world stops and admires me." Barely able to contain his desire, the passionate Marcello begs, "Tie me to my chair!" The others realize what is happening and join in the fun. Her spell has worked and Marcello is soon captivated (*right*).

MIMÌ È TANTO MALATA!

TRACK 11 ACT III On a bitter February dawn, Rodolfo confesses to Marcello: "Mimì is horribly ill." Every day her cough gets worse and she is wasting away. Unknown to Rodolfo, Mimi has overheard him. Realizing that she is dying, she bemoans her fate. Her coughing reveals her and Rodolfo takes her in his arms. Meanwhile, Musetta's shrill laugh is heard from inside the inn and the jealous Marcello rushes back. The two pairs of lovers depict a contrasting picture of romantic love—Mimi and Rodolfo, warm and tender; Marcello and Musetta, fiery and tempestuous.

DORME? RIPOSA.

TRACK 12 ACT IV "Is she sleeping?" Musetta asks. She has just come back with a muff for the dying Mimi. "Just resting," Rodolfo replies, not yet able to face the tragedy ahead. Mimi tenderly receives her gift and gently teases Musetta, "What a spendthrift you are! Thank you." As Rodolfo inquires about the doctor, the others try to reassure him. Musetta prays for Mimi, but Schaunard discovers that she is already dead. A distraught Rodolfo can barely comprehend the situation and his anguished cries ring out, "Mimi!...Mimi!"

Maintaining the Tradition

hen Puccini's third opera, *Manon Lescaut*, was premiered in 1893, Giuseppe Verdi, the reigning genius of Italian opera, was an old man and the public was begininning to wonder who would inherit the maestro's pre-eminent position. With *Manon*, it seemed that Puccini could rightly claim to be the successor. *La Bohème*, Puccini's next opera, fully confirmed him as the heir. Both Verdi and Puccini wrote unforgettable melodies for singers. Like Verdi's *La Traviata*, *La Bohème* is full of memorable tunes—both composers used the human voice to speak directly to the heart. But, above all, Verdi and Puccini had an instinctive sense of drama with which they portayed characters who remain etched into the listener's imagination along with the glorious music they sing.

THE GIRLS IN GRAY

The end of the 19th century saw the first young women working in cities. In Paris, many labored in factories and wore simple gray dresses, and so became known as "grisettes" (from "gris" meaning "gray"). Eventually the word was applied to any young working woman who supported herself independently. With no domestic ties, grisettes were liberated women. From time to time, they could be shrewd about who they took as lovers to support them, but they were not seen as prostitutes or courtesans. Grisettes followed their hearts and whims and gave themselves freely for love or pleasure.

ECLIPSING THE GODS

The first performance of *La Bohème* was on February 1, 1896 at the Teatro Regio in Turin, conducted by the 28-year-old Arturo Toscanini. At first, the opera was not received enthusiastically, perhaps because it followed a production of Wagner's *Twilight of the Gods* and the critics found it difficult to shift their sympathies from the metaphysical struggles of Teutonic deities to those of young Parisians with no fixed morals. Puccini was heartbroken. In about three months, however, the opera had become immensely popular. It was shown in Rome, then Naples and Palermo, where it was ecstatically received. Within three years, it was performed all over the world: from South America to Egypt. In England, following performances sung in English by the Carl Rosa Company, the great soprano, Nellie Melba, sang the role of Mimi in Italian at Covent Garden. Today, *La Bohème* vies with *Carmen* and *Aida* as one of the most performed operas.

GREAT PERFORMERS

La Bohème goes in and out of fashion with critics but is never unsuccessful at the box office. In its early years, the role of Rodolfo was associated with the great tenor, Enrico Caruso. Toscanini was still conducting the opera in legendary performances in New York 50 years after the premiere; and in recent years, Luciano Pavarotti made Rodolfo one of his staple roles in the opera house (*far left*, with Gino Quicilico as Marcello). Particularly famous Mimis since World War II have included the world-reknown Renata Tebaldi and Renata Scotto.

KEY NOTES

The 1996 Tony-award winning Broadway musical Rent is a loosely based adaptation of Puccini's La Bohème. The themes are remarkably similar with Rent having a more modern day topic set in New York City.

Lucia di Lammermoor

GAETANO DONIZETTI *1797–1848*

*L*ucia di Lammermoor is the story of "The Bride of Lammermoor" and her ill-fated lover, Edgardo. Lucia captures the audience's sympathy from the beginning. Under intense emotional pressure, she loses her mind in the "Mad Scene" that is one of opera's most famous.

PEAK OF SUCCESS

Donizetti had already written 50 stage works and was one of Europe's most popular opera composers when he was asked to write *Lucia di Lammermoor* for the Teatro San Carlo in Naples. Unfortunately, the San Carlo was run by the grossly incompetent Royal Commission, and at one time it looked as though the opera was doomed. The Commission continually stalled over both the text and choice of librettists, and by the time it gave the go-ahead, the project was well behind schedule. Donizetti, however, was determined and responded by composing the score in just

six weeks, but problems still continued.

The first Lucia, Fanny Tacchinardi-Persiani, refused to sing after the Commission failed to pay her. Donizetti wrote, "Crisis is at hand. The public is fed up. The Commission is about to be dissolved. Vesuvius is smoking and the eruption is near." Fortunately, Donizetti's pessimism was ill-founded and the opera eventually premiered only two months late, on September 26, 1835 to huge acclaim. The great French tenor, Gilbert Duprez, took the part of Edgardo. He is called the first "modern" tenor for his technique of voice projection.

A Family Feud

This tale of star-crossed love is set in late 17th-century Scotland. There has long been an angry feud between the Ashton and Ravenswood families. Enrico Ashton is now out of political favor and wants to force his sister, Lucia, into a marriage that will restore his position. But she loves another—the family's bitter enemy, Edgardo.

PRINCIPAL CHARACTERS

Lucia: main character;
Edgardo Ravenswood: her lover;
Enrico Ashton: Lucia's brother; **Raimondo:** a chaplain; **Arturo:** the bridegroom chosen for Lucia; **Normanno:** Enrico's huntsman

SECRET MEETINGS

ACT I

At Ravenswood Castle (*left*), Enrico Ashton meets up with Normanno, who tells him that Lucia has been secretly meeting his enemy, Edgardo Ravenswood. She is clearly in love with him. Enrico, determined that Lucia shall make an alliance to redeem the family fortunes, goes into a horrible fit of rage. Later that evening, Lucia awaits her lover by a haunted fountain. She is full of foreboding about their future. Edgardo arrives to tell her he must leave for France on diplomatic business and he wants to ask Enrico openly for her hand. Terrified of the consequences, Lucia refuses to let him do so. They exchange rings and pledge their love to each other with the most solemn vows.

FAMILY DECEPTION

ACT II

Months have passed. Edgardo's and Lucia's love letters have been intercepted, and Enrico has arranged for Lucia to marry Arturo, a wealthy lord. He plans to trick her into agreeing to the wedding by showing her a forged letter implying that Edgardo has found another love. Helpless, distraught and under intense pressure, Lucia gives in. Later, the wedding guests assemble in the great hall (*right*). But just as Lucia is married to Arturo, Edgardo bursts in. On seeing the signed wedding contract, he curses Lucia for her apparent faithlessness. Throwing her ring at her feet, he snatches back his own and flees.

THE "MAD SCENE"

ACT III

Edgardo is in his ruined home at Wolf's Crag. Enrico appears and torments him by telling him that Lucia is even now enjoying her wedding night. The two men swear to fight a duel the next day, each determined to avenge their families and kill the other. At the wedding feast, the merriment is ended abruptly by Raimondo who reports the shocking news that Lucia has lost her mind and killed Arturo. Lucia enters. In her madness, she vocalizes the thoughts in her unhinged mind, imagining that she is talking to her lover, Edgardo, seeing the ghost that haunts the

fountain, and marrying her true love. She asks the guests to shed bitter tears on her grave, before collapsing, more dead than alive. As Edgardo hears the news of Lucia's terrible breakdown, the bell tolls her death. Devastated, he stabs himself (*above*), yearning to be united with Lucia in heaven.

Betrayal and Tragedy

AH! VERRANNO A TE SULL' AURE

TRACK 13 · ACT I

In this touching duet, Lucia and Edgardo, having met secretly at the haunted fountain, speak of their fated, desperate love. They swear fidelity before heaven (*right*), and exchange rings. Unfortunately, Edgardo has been called away to France and they bid a heart-rending farewell. Lucia says she will be sustained if from time to time she receives a letter from him. "Ah!" she exclaims, "My sighs will come to you borne on gentle breezes." Edgardo joins in and together they sing that the seas will echo their laments, and that they will be true to their pledge of love.

CHI MI FRENA IN TAL MOMENTO?

TRACK 14 · ACT II

Having been tricked into marriage, Lucia is horrified when Edgardo bursts in just as she has signed the wedding contract. All the principal characters: Lucia, Edgardo, Enrico, Raimondo, Normanno and Alisa (Lucia's maid) begin to express their feelings of anger, remorse, horror and terror. "Who can restrain me in such a moment?" they sing. This is one of the most famous ensembles in all opera, building from a duet to a quartet and finally a sextet with chorus (*left*). In the early days of the gramophone, it was recorded by the legendary Enrico Caruso in the role of Edgardo.

MAD SCENE: OH GIUSTO CIELO!

 Deceived by her family and unjustly spurned by Edgardo because of her apparent faithlessness, Lucia has become deranged and has stabbed her husband, Arturo, to death. She now reappears among the wedding guests, dishevelled and deathly pale. "Oh, merciful heavens!" they gasp, "She looks as if she has risen from the grave." Lucia imagines that she is talking to Edgardo by the haunted fountain, "Alas! The terrible specter rises and parts us," she cries, then enacts a marriage to him and the trauma of his rejection. "I was a sacrifice of my cruel brother, but I have always loved you," she swears.

 Famously, her aria is accompanied by a flute that matches the purity of her singing. When Joan Sutherland sang the role, she acted as if the notes of the flute were birds, and chased them around the stage.

WOMEN ON THE VERGE

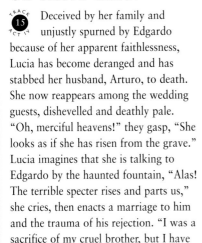 The woman driven to distraction through unrequited love often occurs in literature. Perhaps the most famous is Ophelia (*portrayed below*) in Shakespeare's Hamlet, who drowns herself in despair. It was also a feature of 19th-century operas for the heroine to become unhinged for the same reason, playing out her desperate state with her most brilliant singing technique, and evoking the audience's sympathy. The "Mad Scene" in *Lucia* is most famous of all such scenes, but Donizetti had already set the standard in *Anna Bolena*, when the Queen of England goes mad at the thought of her impending execution. Composers even vied with each other in inventing variations on the mad scene. In *Elvira of I Puritani*, Bellini created a heroine who keeps veering between madness and sanity, so giving his audience several mad scenes in the course of one opera.

The Reluctant Bride

*D*onizetti's opera is based on "The Bride of Lammermoor," a novel by Sir Walter Scott (*left*), published in 1819. A prolific writer, Scott had a huge readership at home and in Europe. Most of his stories were vividly historical and set in England or his native Scotland, which seemed a wild and fascinating place to mainland Europeans. His characters were realistic, with a strong dash of nobility or villainy, and his subjects picturesque and dramatic—ideal for stage adaptations. Opera composers, always seeking a strong storyline, often seized on his narratives, much like turning classics into films or television serials today. This particular story gave rise to four operas, of which Donizetti's *Lucia di Lammermoor* is the only one to have survived.

MARRIAGE OF CONVENIENCE

The historical Lucy of Scott's story (*portrayed right*) was Janet Dalrymple, a Viscount's daughter, forced into a dynastic marriage to David Dunbar of Baldoon in 1669. Janet's real love, Archibald, Lord Rutherford, did not turn up to save her and the bride went insane. She stabbed the groom, spoke one final sentence, "Take up your bonny bridegroom," and died two weeks later. The groom recovered, but refused to speak of what happened. Scott probably heard the story from his mother, who was a Rutherford. He moved the drama to Rutherford country, the Lammermoors or Lammermuir Hills, south of Edinburgh. In his novel—as in real life—the evil genius is the mother, a steely hearted woman of terrifying ambition. In the opera, Lucia's tough family member becomes the nasty brother, Enrico.

IN PERFORMANCE

The first Lucia, Fanny Tacchinardi-Persiani, also performed the role in Vienna and London, setting a strong singing and acting style. It has been a favorite role of the greatest sopranos, including Adelina Patti and Nellie Melba. In 1931, Lily Pons made a sensational debut in New York as Lucia, singing the "Mad Scene" a tone higher than written. In the 1950s, the legendary Maria Callas brought a fresh interpretation, expressing the various moods of Lucia with immense pathos. In 1959, the Australian Joan Sutherland (*above*) sang the part with incredible beauty of tone in a dazzling production by Franco Zeffirelli in London, and around the world. These latter two divas helped revive interest in opera overall, especially Donizetti's operas.

CHILD OF THE THEATER

The Neapolitan Salvatore Cammarano (*below*), the librettist for *Lucia*, was born in 1801 into a gifted artistic and theatrical family. He trained as a painter but began writing successfully for the theater in his late teens. He was a scene-painter, then producer, then poet at the Teatro San Carlo, where he met Donizetti and formed a successful partnership, writing seven more operas with him. Cammarano followed the contemporary fashion for colorful drama, and Verdi admired his gift for conjuring up a scene in words. Cammarano wrote many librettos for him, including *Luisa Miller* and *Il Trovatore*, unfinished at his death in 1852.

KEY NOTES

In one production of Lucia in New York, Maria Callas was singing a duet with an Italian baritone, who held a high note longer than required, presumably to show off. "Basta!" she said in Italian—meaning "enough," but it was unfortunately misheard by those nearby.

Credits & Acknowledgments

PICTURE CREDITS

Cover /Title and Contents Pages/ IBC: Fine Art Photographic Library/Graham Gallery (Sir Frank Dicksee: Juliet's Last Thoughts) Arena Images/Ron Scherl 5(t), 17, 22(l); Bridgeman Art Library, London/Private Collection (Egisto Lancerotto: An Entertaining Evening) 4(t), Chris Beetles Ltd., London (John Simmons: By the Window) 5(b), Bibliothèque Nationale, Paris (Georges Labadie Pilotell: Caricature of Verdi) 8(r), State Russian Museum, St. Petersburg (Vasili Maksimovich Maksimov: Dreaming of the Future) 10 & 12(l), Galleria d'Arte Moderna, Florence (Giovanni Fattori: Self Portrait) 14(l), University of Dundee, Scotland (Thomas Miles Richardson: Tarbert Castle, Loch Fyne) 20(t), Forbes Magazine Collection, New York (Sir William Quiller Orchardson: Queen of the Swords) 21(r), Christie's, London (John William Waterhouse: Ophelia) 23(l), Scottish National Portrait Gallery, Edinburgh (Sir William Allan: Sir Walter Scott) 24(l), City of Bristol Museum and Art Gallery (Sir John Everett Millais: The Bride of Lammermoor) 24(r); Jean-Loup Charmet: 11; Giancarlo Costa: 3, 13(r), 16(r), 19(l), 22(r); Mary Evans Picture Library: 9(r); Fine Art Photographic Library/By Courtesy of Cambridge Fine Art (Thomas Herbert Maguire: Vanity Fair) 14(r),Waterhouse & Dodd (Alfred Augustus Glendening Jnr.: A Parisian Flower Seller) 16(l); Lebrecht Collection: 8(l), 25(r); Performing Arts Library/Clive Barda 2, 4(b), 23(r); Photostage/Donald Cooper 7(r); Reg Wilson: 6, 7(l), 9(l), 12(r), 13(l), 15(r & l), 18, 20(b), 21(l), 25(l).

All illustrations and symbols: John See